Baby Animals™

Seals • Focas

ALICE TWINE

TRADUCCIÓN AL ESPAÑOL:
José María Obregón

PowerKiDS press & **Editorial Buenas Letras**™
New York

For Nora and Annie Quesnell and Hailey Power

Published in 2008 by The Rosen Publishing Group, Inc.
29 East 21st Street, New York, NY 10010

First Edition

Editor: Amelie von Zumbusch
Book Design: Julio Gil
Layout Design: Lissette González
Photo Researcher: Nicole Pristash

Photo Credits: Cover, p. 1 © Norbert Rosing/Getty Images; p. 5 © SuperStock, Inc.; pp. 7, 9, 11, 13, 15, 17, 19, 21, 23, 24 (top left, top right, bottom left, bottom right) © www.shutterstock.com.

Cataloging Data

Twine, Alice.
  Seals / Alice Twine; traducción al español: José María Obregón. — 1st ed.
    p. cm. — (Baby animals–Animales bebé)
  Includes index.
  ISBN-13: 978-1-4042-7632-1 (lib. bdg.)
  ISBN-10: 1-4042-7632-7 (lib. bdg.)
  1. Seals (Animals)—Infancy—Juvenile literature. 2. Spanish Language Materials I. Title.

Manufactured in the United States of America.

Websites: Due to the changing nature of Internet links, PowerKids Press and Buenas Letras have developed an online list of Web sites related to the subject of this book. This site is updated regularly. Please use this link to access the list: www.powerkidslinks.com/baby/seals/

Contents

Contenido

Baby seals are called pups. Mother seals take good care of their pups. Seal pups drink their mother's milk.

A las focas bebé se les llama cachorros. Las mamás foca cuidan muy bien a sus cachorros y los alimentan con su leche.

4

Seals are good swimmers. They use their back **flippers** to push themselves through the water.

Las focas son muy buenas para nadar. Las focas usan las **aletas** traseras para moverse en el agua.

6

7

Some seal pups can swim when they are first born. Other seal pups learn to swim when they are several weeks old.

Algunos cachorros pueden nadar desde que nacen. Otros cachorros aprenden a nadar varias semanas después.

 8

Seal pups can dive down hundreds of feet (m) under water. However, they have to come up to the **surface** to breathe.

Los cachorros de foca pueden bucear bajo el agua cientos de pies (m). Cuando bucean tienen que salir a la **superficie** para respirar.

Most seal pups are born on beaches. Some pups live on a beach with a seal **colony** for several months after they are born.

La mayoría de las focas nace en las playas. Algunas de ellas viven en una **colonia** de focas por varios meses después de nacidas.

13

There are many kinds of seals.
This pup is a harbor seal.
Harbor seals are also called
common seals.

Hay muchos tipos de focas.
Esta es una foca de puerto.
A la foca de puerto también
se le llama foca común.

14

15

Baby harp seals, like this pup, have white fur. As a harp seal grows up, its **coat** will turn darker.

Las foca arpa, como este cachorro, tienen **pelaje** blanco. Cuando las focas arpa crecen, el pelaje se hace más oscuro.

This pup is an elephant seal. Elephant seals are the biggest kind of seal. They can grow up to 15 feet (5 m) long.

Este es un cachorro de elefante marino, las focas más grandes. Los elefantes marinos pueden tener hasta 15 pies (5 m) de largo.

18

Baby sea lions are also called pups. Sea lions are related to seals. Unlike seals, sea lions can walk on their front flippers.

A los bebés de los leones marinos también se les llama cachorros. Los leones marinos son parientes de las focas. Los leones marinos pueden caminar con sus aletas.

This is an eared seal. Eared seals have "seal" in their name, but they are not true seals. They are more like sea lions.

Este es un lobo marino. A los lobos marinos también se les llama osos marinos. Los lobos marinos son más parecidos a los leones marinos que a las focas.

Words to Know • Palabras que debes saber

coat / (el) pelaje

colony / (la) colonia

flipper / (la) aleta

surface / (la) superficie